# The ADHD Teen Survival Guide

# by the same author

**ADHD Is Our Superpower**
The Amazing Talents and Skills
of Children with ADHD
**Soli Lazarus**
Illustrated by Adriana Camargo
ISBN 978 1 78775 730 1
eISBN 978 1 78775 731 8

# of related interest

**The Teenage Girl's Guide to
Living Well with ADHD**
Improve Your Self-Esteem, Self-Care
and Self Knowledge
**Sonia Ali**
ISBN 978 1 78775 768 4
eISBN 978 1 78775 769 1

**ADHD an A-Z**
Figuring It Out Step by Step
**Leanne Maskell**
ISBN 978 1 83997 385 7
eISBN 978 1 83997 386 4

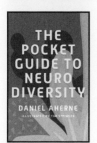

**The Pocket Guide to Neurodiversity**
**Daniel Aherne**
Illustrated by Tim Stringer
ISBN 978 1 83997 014 6
eISBN 978 1 83997 015 3

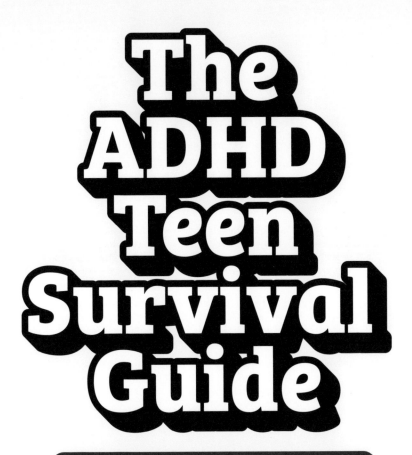

# The ADHD Teen Survival Guide

## Your Launchpad to an Amazing Life

### Soli Lazarus

**Designed and Illustrated
by Kara McHale**

**Jessica Kingsley Publishers**
London and Philadelphia

First published in Great Britain in 2025 by Jessica Kingsley Publishers
An imprint of John Murray Press

1

Copyright © Soli Lazarus 2025

Front cover image source: Kara McHale
Afterword for Parents Copyright © Peter Hill 2025

*The information contained in this book is not intended to replace the services
of trained medical professionals or to be a substitute for medical advice. You
are advised to consult a doctor on any matters relating to your health, and in
particular on any matters that may require diagnosis or medical attention.*

The fonts, layout and overall design of this book have been prepared
according to dyslexia-friendly principles. At JKP we aim to make our
books' content accessible to as many readers as possible.

A CIP catalogue record for this title is available from the
British Library and the Library of Congress

ISBN 978 1 83997 663 6
eISBN 978 1 83997 664 3

Printed and bound in China by Leo Paper Products Ltd

Jessica Kingsley Publishers' policy is to use papers that are natural,
renewable and recyclable products and made from wood grown in
sustainable forests. The logging and manufacturing processes are expected
to conform to the environmental regulations of the country of origin.

Jessica Kingsley Publishers
Carmelite House
50 Victoria Embankment
London EC4Y 0DZ

www.jkp.com

John Murray Press
Part of Hodder & Stoughton Ltd
An Hachette Company

# Thank you to the superstars who helped me with this book:

Jack, Daisy, Fern, Hollie, Donny, Eoghan, Matt, Callum, Raphie, Grace, Daniel, Coby, Woody, Ziyaad, Dave, Leon, Patrick, William, Joel, Dorian Ray, Tamzin, Ashleigh, Max, Lexi

# CONTENTS

# Why Have I Written This Book?

**My name is Soli and I help and support families with teenagers with ADHD (attention deficit hyperactivity disorder).**

I was a teacher for 30 years so I know what teachers could be doing to help you. My son has ADHD and so I have a good idea what could help you at home too.

**But why have I written this book?**

When you were given your ADHD diagnosis, would you have liked an explanation about the condition and some stuff adults could do to help you? Yup, that's why I wrote this book.

I asked teenagers, just like you, to tell me about their experiences. I asked them about some common issues that I think may be affecting your life. Things like friends, school, organisation and home life. Then I asked them what the adults could do to help.

I was really blown away and humbled by their responses. These young people knew exactly what should be happening.

I hope this book gives you the confidence to use your voice to let the adults know how they can help you.

Keep in touch.

*Soli*

soli@yellow-sun.com

# The
# Aim
# of
# This
# Book

**The aim of this book is to give you a voice.**

I want you to know and understand what ADHD is, and how it may affect you. **You can have an amazing life and this book could be the launchpad for you—where you not only survive but you soar and thrive.**

Getting a diagnosis of ADHD may give you an explanation of why you behave like you do, why you find it hard to do some stuff, why your emotions may be all over the place, why you find it hard to concentrate and maybe make friends.

# You are NOT broken and you DO NOT need to be fixed.

But with kindness, help and support you can have an amazing and successful life.

And you can politely let people know what you need.

# You have a voice...

If you explain to adults what you need and they listen to you, then this will be much easier for you. Right?

**So let's get started...**

# CHAPTER ONE

# WHAT IS ADHD?

First of all, let's be clear about ADHD.

## It is NOT a made-up condition to excuse so-called naughty boys in classrooms or poor parenting.

ADHD is a neurological condition and is real. This means it is a condition that affects the brain. We can prove this by using magnetic resonance imaging (MRI) scans to show how an ADHD brain looks different and behaves differently to other brains.[1]

**ADHD has been around for centuries, affects both boys and girls, and is prevalent in people from all sectors of society and all around the world.**

By the way, many people don't like this description as

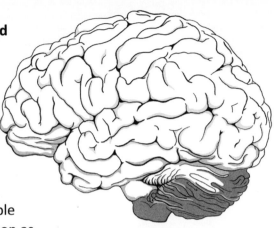

# YOU DON'T HAVE a deficit of attention—YOU ACTUALLY HAVE too much attention,

GRATIFICATION

you're distracted and find it hard to pay attention to things you don't find stimulating, interesting or motivating. This may be to do with the part of the brain that seeks reward and immediate gratification.

Many people describe ADHD as like having numerous computer tabs open in your brain or tons of TVs all playing at once. It must be exhausting to work out which one to focus on.

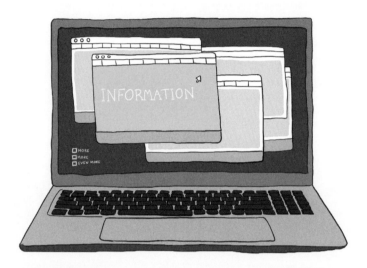

Many people don't like the word **disordered** either—which sounds like something is broken or damaged. You are definitely not disordered—your brain is wired differently which gives you certain skills and a unique way of thinking.

### Perhaps ADHD should be renamed "attention dynamic hyperactive difference".

### Or something else... What do you think?

Or maybe abandon the acronym altogether and classify the condition as **neurodivergent** alongside other neuro-differences such as dyslexia, dyspraxia, dyscalculia, dysgraphia, Tourette's and autism.

By the way, if you have been diagnosed with ADHD you are likely to have one of these other conditions as well.

One of the main causes of ADHD is **genetics**. Which means someone in your family may also have ADHD. Perhaps a parent, grandparent, aunt or cousin.

**So here's a bit of sciency stuff...**

The neurons in your brain have an important role. They receive messages from external stimuli from the environment and then send signals to the areas of the brain that control emotions, behaviour, sensory information, learning and movement.

You have about 86 billion of these neurons in your brain. A massive number which is hard to visualise.

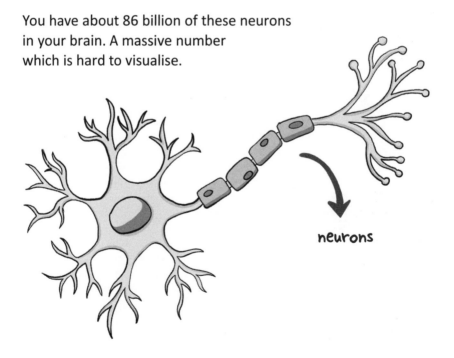

neurons

To make it easier to comprehend this number, let's swap the word **neurons** for **pixels**.

Imagine a TV has 2,000,000 (2 million) pixels.

Stack 200 TVs on top of each other which is the same height as Big Ben in London. There would be 400,000,000.

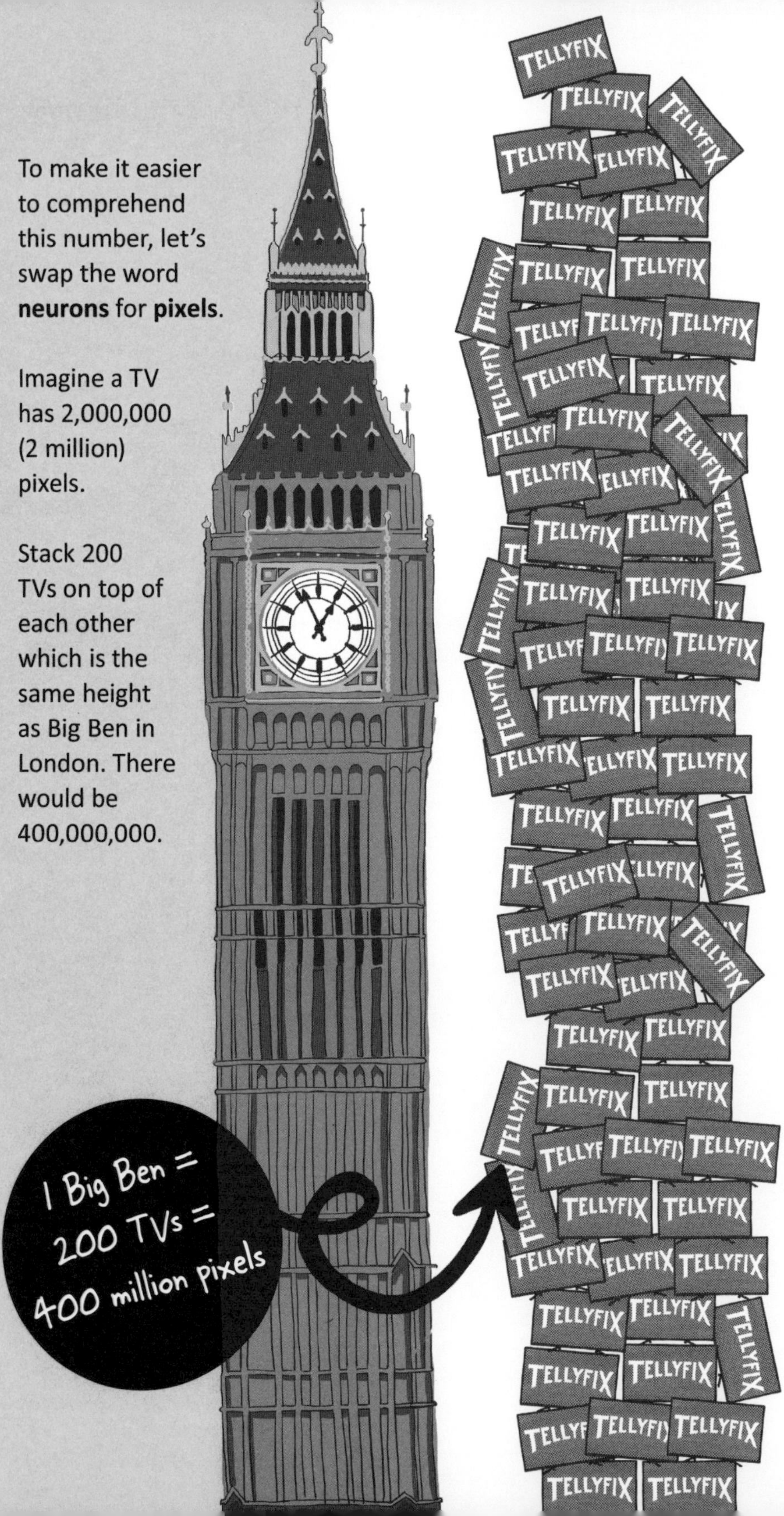

I Big Ben =
200 TVs =
400 million pixels

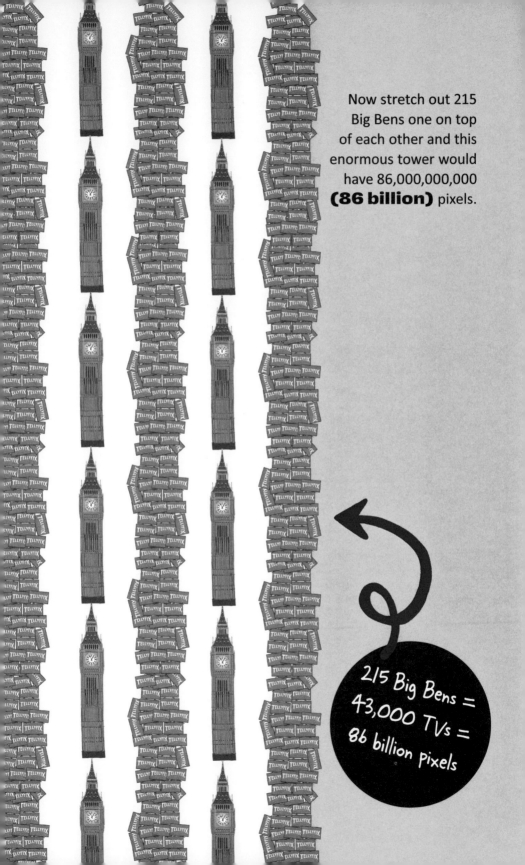

Now stretch out 215 Big Bens one on top of each other and this enormous tower would have 86,000,000,000 **(86 billion)** pixels.

215 Big Bens =
43,000 TVs =
86 billion Pixels

But in an ADHD brain these 86 billion neurons are not behaving consistently. They should be regularly firing their electrical charge to the chemical neurotransmitters which are dopamine, serotonin and noradrenaline.

neurotransmitters

If there is a lack of these chemical neurotransmitters, then the signals don't get through to neighbouring neurons and so the brain does not receive the information.

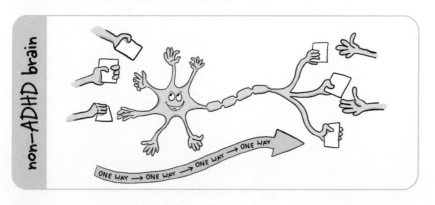

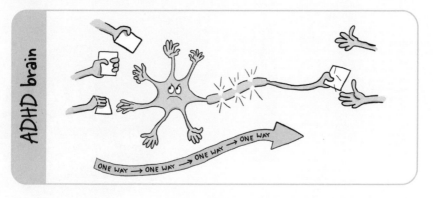

Remember the role of a neuron is to help control emotions, behaviour, sensory information, learning and movement.

So if the chemistry of your brain means the signals are not reaching their destination, then it is no wonder sometimes you struggle to do the things other people find easy—like focusing and concentrating.

But here is the clever bit...an ADHD brain is naturally seeking out the release of these chemical neurotransmitters, particularly dopamine, through experiencing rewards, stimulation and excitement. It's like an ADHD brain knows it is lacking the chemicals, so naturally attempts to create the chemical release. Smart, eh?

So you may find that you are seeking immediate satisfaction like going on a rollercoaster, buying a new video game, eating cake, getting a deep massage or winding up your younger sibling.

But a long-term project, doing homework or tidying your room creates no chemical release of neurotransmitters, as there is no reward or pleasure, so your brain gets distracted.

**We know that medication, exercise, diet and sleep can help these pesky neurotransmitters to fire more consistently.**

Another interesting thing is what's going on in the **amygdala**.

The amygdala in an ADHD brain is often in a heightened state of **fight or flight**.

This means you may be extremely alert and distracted by things in the environment a lot of the time.

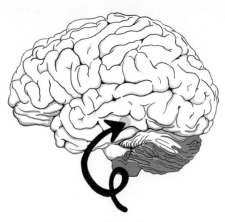

warning signs from the amygdala

This would be great if you lived in prehistoric times. You would be alert and would notice the sabre-toothed tiger approaching and you would be ready.

The non-ADHD cave person, however, would be focusing on roasting the antelope's leg in the firepit and would not notice the sabre-toothed tiger until it was too late...

Unfortunately for ADHDers, you have to cope with the institution of school which expects you to do all the things your brain finds challenging like sit still, focus on boring stuff and keep your ideas quiet.

# Grrrrr!
# This may be why school is not your happiest place...

# CHAPTER TWO

# SUPERPOWER

**Now the good news...**

Your unique brain chemistry means that your brain has the power of a Ferrari engine—but with bicycle brakes (thank you Dr Ned Halliwell for that analogy).

This means your brain is whirring at 200 miles an hour but you find it hard to slow down the thoughts.

Some well-known people have been diagnosed with ADHD including will.i.am, Lewis Hamilton, Simone Biles, Nicola Adams, Zayn Malik, Loyle Carner and Ben Whittaker.

There are tons more well-known people in sport, media, business, politics and the arts.

And look how successful they are.

They have used their ADHD to push themselves forward.

**And you can too.**

> # "ADHD can mean you get to an idea quicker, you can think out of the box, you can make connections."
>
> **Rory Bremner, Comedian**

This means that you think in a unique way. Different from your peers. So you can solve a problem because your brain is coming up with different ideas that may get to the solution. Yup. Rory explains it well.

**So what are the positives?**

It may not feel like it at the moment, but if you can see yourself as having "superpowers" then you can flip the way others respond to you.

Shout it out loud and let's get rid of the stigma where people think that ADHD is a made-up excuse.

# Having ADHD can be a gift.

And this is why...

**Fearless**
Your brain is not weighing up the risks before you do something, which means you just go for it and may discover a new experience or way of doing something that no one else has thought of before.

**Observant**
You notice everything as you are distracted by what is going on around you. This can often be more interesting than the task in front of you which is not stimulating your brain. This means you are super observant and will notice things other people miss.

**Determined**
You can get stuck in a thought or idea and this means that once you want to do something, you will keep going until it is done.

**Energetic**
You have tons of energy whether that's externally or internally. You can keep going when everybody else stops. Often this could be through the night...

**Intuitive**
Adults may say you have a "sixth sense" because you are noticing what is going on and so you may have a gift for instinctively getting something right.

**Curious**
You want to know why and will pursue an answer until you are satisfied. This can mean you may discover new ways of doing things or be able to teach yourself a new skill.

| | |
|---|---|
| **Fairness**<br>Because you are observant you notice when things are fair or unfair. This means you have a strong sense of justice. | **Humour**<br>You are seriously funny as you can notice the nuance in a situation, mimic people's mannerisms and have a free spirit that doesn't inhibit you. |
| **Creative**<br>Your brain is buzzing with stuff. You will often think of a unique way of doing things that no one else has thought of. Go you! | **Hyper-focus**<br>When you are highly motivated and interested in something (or if it is urgent) you can apply all your time and attention and get it done. |
| **Excited**<br>You can get incredibly exuberant and excited which can be infectious and empowering to those around you. | **Problem solver**<br>Your brain is so full of ideas, when a problem arises, you don't stop and think and waste time trying to think of solutions—you just react and sort out the problem quickly. |
| **Compassion**<br>Because you are aware of everything going on, you can show amazing empathy for those around you who may be hurt or sad. You are a loyal friend. | **Entrepreneur**<br>Many successful business owners have ADHD as your brain thinks in a clever, unique way, you have tons of energy, you don't give up and you are determined to get things done. |

# CHAPTER THREE

# IMPACT ON YOUR LIFE

**Now the tricky bit.**

Having ADHD means there may be an impact on your day-to-day life.

It may feel like a brick wall is in your way, stopping you from living a good life.

This may be a bit sad to read—but don't worry, we will come up with some solutions later in this book and break down that wall.

**So you may have challenges with...**

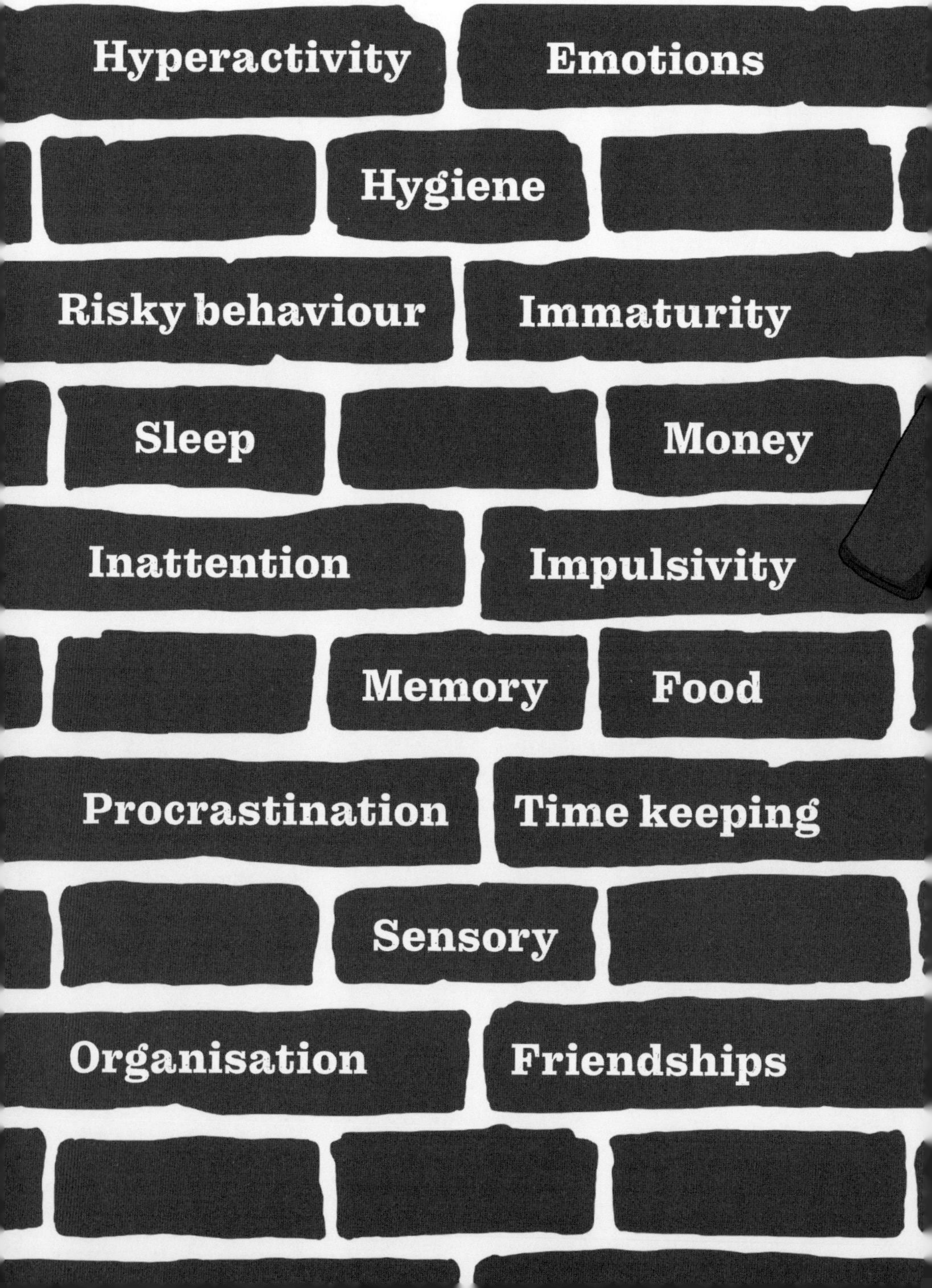

Hyperactivity

Emotions

Hygiene

Risky behaviour

Immaturity

Sleep

Money

Inattention

Impulsivity

Memory

Food

Procrastination

Time keeping

Sensory

Organisation

Friendships

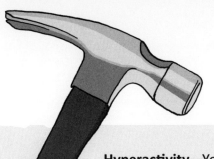

**Hyperactivity**—You need to move, fidget, doodle, stim—in fact anything that keeps your brain motivated.

**Emotions**—You get emotionally overwhelmed quickly and need time to calm down so you can refocus. You may get worried and stuck in a thought. You may have feelings of failure and being rejected.

**Hygiene**—You may find washing extremely boring.

**Risky behaviour**—Your brain craves stimulation and excitement which you may find in risky activities that could be dangerous or unlawful.

**Immaturity**—You may be socially and emotionally lagging behind your peers.[2]

**Sleep**—Your brain is buzzing which may make it difficult to sleep. Also night time may be too quiet and calm with no distractions so it's tempting to stay up. But then you're tired in the morning.

**Money**—You may find it hard to save and manage your money as the instant gratification of spending is extremely rewarding.

**Inattention**—You may lose focus and get lost in the thoughts in your head—so you may miss stuff that is being said.

**Impulsivity**—You may do something before you have time to think if it's a good idea.

**Memory**—Because your brain is constantly full, you do not pay attention to the things you don't think are important. So you forget them quickly.

**Food**—Your medication may be affecting your appetite or you may be reluctant to try new flavours or textures.

**Procrastination**—You may put off anything that doesn't interest or excite you.

**Time keeping**—You misjudge time and can be late or way too early.

**Sensory**—You may be sensitive to things in the environment that make you feel uncomfortable. Smells, sounds, movement and the feel of things on your skin.

**Organisation**—You don't pay attention to where things are placed as it may not be important to you. You then can't find things when you need them.

**Friendships**—You may lose friends because they don't understand ADHD. You may talk a lot, interrupt, be unreliable or be inappropriate. You then feel rejected.

But with help, you can overcome these challenges and smash down that wall...

# In your life, focus on the positives or "superpowers".

Understand that you may need to do things a bit differently or may need those around you to respond in a different way.

It doesn't mean you are bad, lazy or stupid.

It doesn't mean you are deliberately trying to wind up your family, teachers or friends.

It just means that people around you need to understand you and be kind.

**School can be a troubling place for someone with ADHD.**

The rules and expectations surrounding school are so hard.

Stuff like:

* Sitting quietly

* Listening for long periods of time

* Waiting your turn

* Subjects you find boring and unstimulating

* Wearing uniform

Plus it's the only place where you are lumped together with people of exactly your age and expected to get on with them.

## Grrrrr. No wonder school fails so many young people with ADHD.

**Home may be tricky too as there may be conflict over stuff like:**

* Getting on with siblings

* Screens

* Phone

* Food

* Bedtime

* Homework

* Going out

On top of all of this ADHD stuff, you may already be experiencing hormonal changes (because that's what happens to all teenage bodies).

So life at the moment may feel pretty rubbish (insert other words that fit how you feel...).

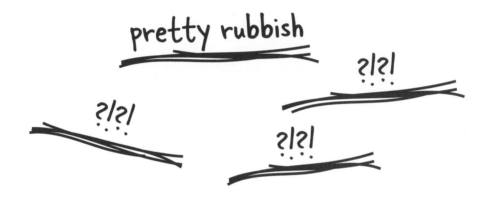

But remember, I want to help you and empower you, so that you know how your ADHD brain works, what you can ask for and how people around you can help.

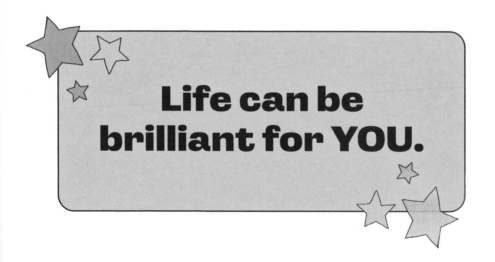

**Life can be brilliant for YOU.**

# CHAPTER FOUR

# MEDICATION

I wanted to devote a separate chapter to medication as this subject comes up a lot in my support groups and there are always many questions.

Once you have been diagnosed you may be offered medication. There is evidence that medication is highly effective and can help manage the difficulties you experience with your ADHD brain. But of course, you and your family may decide not to use medication. Which is absolutely okay.[3]

Please note, I am not medically trained so I can only give factual information and cannot give personal advice or recommendations.

I highly recommend *The Parents' Guide to ADHD Medicines* by Professor Peter Hill.[4]

I have used this book for reference in this chapter and all statements are based on his experience and research.

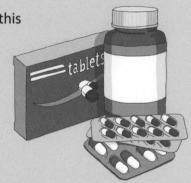

I am delighted that Professor Hill has also contributed to this book by providing the Afterword for Parents.

# ADHD Q&A

**Question: What does the medication do?**
**Answer**: ADHD medication increases the chemical neurotransmitters in the brain to allow the neurons to fire consistently. This helps you with focus, impulsivity and emotions.

**Question: Will medication take away my ADHD?**
**Answer**: No. Medication only works whilst it is in your system. It is recommended that alongside medication you also use adjustments, specific strategies, have a great sleep routine, eat a high protein diet and include plenty of exercise.

**Question: What are the different types of medication?**
**Answer**: ADHD medication can be in the form of stimulants or non-stimulants. They can be short-acting or long-acting. The prescribing clinician will monitor you closely to work out the best type and dose for you.

**Question: Will I need to be seen again by the prescribing clinician?**
**Answer**: Yes. You should be seen regularly by the clinician who will monitor weight, blood pressure and the effectiveness of the medicine. Your parents should keep a diary noting focus, sleep, mood and food intake.

**Question: What are the short-term effects?**
**Answer**: Medication will only have an effect whilst it is active in your system. It can however affect mood, appetite and sleep. These effects can be alleviated with careful monitoring and changing doses or type of medication.

# ADHD Q&A

**Question: Will I be turned into a zombie?**
**Answer**: No, not if you are taking the right medication at the right dose.

**Question: What happens if I want to stop?**
**Answer**: You just stop. There is no evidence of any long-term damage or effects to the brain when taking or stopping the medication.

**Question: Is the ADHD medication addictive?**
**Answer**: No. There is no evidence that you will become addicted.

**Question: What do I say to people who ask why I am taking the medication?**
**Answer**: You tell them that ADHD is a neurological condition and the medication helps your brain. Remember...

# YOU ARE NOT DAMAGED, ILL OR BROKEN.

# Listen to Our Voices

In this next part of this book are suggestions and solutions to some of the challenges you may be experiencing. You may want to share some of these things with the adults in your life so that **you** can make change happen. Encourage them to listen to your voice

# because your voice matters!

Finally, if you feel things are getting too much, please speak to a trusted adult and tell them how you feel. There are contact details at the back of the book that you may find helpful too.

**I asked teenagers, just like you, what they found difficult.**

↳ **Then I asked them what would help them.**

↳ **Why those things would work.**

↳ **And what to avoid.**

↳ **This is what they said...**

# CHAPTER FIVE

# SCHOOL

**As I said earlier, being at school can be really tricky for young people with ADHD.**

It's really sad because school could be a fantastic place for you to jump on opportunities to thrive.

School could be a place where you discover your love of science, history, sport, drama, music. There are tons of chances to be amazing and show your creativity, your curiosity and problem-solving skills.

But if the adults don't understand what you need, then you may be experiencing an environment that feels hostile, punitive and unkind. **I bet you are totally fed up with getting into trouble, detentions and exclusions.**

**So be the voice.**

# Quick Wins

* Know what things help you in each lesson.

* Politely communicate this to each teacher at the start of the lesson. You may want to write it out in a list.

* You could ask for small steps instructions written on post-its, to sit where there are no distractions, visual reminders or prompts, movement breaks, use of a laptop or voice recorder, and a copy of slides and a highlighter pen.

* Request extra time in tests or take a test in a separate room so there are no distractions and you can "stop the clock" for a movement break.

* You may need to have all your equipment organised in one place in each subject classroom so there is less for you to remember to pack.

* You could have extra copies of textbooks in school so that you can leave a set at home.

* The use of a timer is really visual and may help you in each lesson to pace yourself.

* You may need opportunities to present your work in a different way.

* Using sensory equipment helps you focus and concentrate.

* Ask to see an example of a good piece of work, so you know exactly what to aim for.

# Quick Wins

* You may need adjustments with the uniform policy or behaviour policy.

* Find the adult in school who gets you. This can be your "go to" person if things get too much or you need someone to talk to.

* Involve yourself in activities that you enjoy—this may be the reason and incentive for you to go to school.

* Have a plan for lunchtimes if you feel lonely. Maybe you can help younger children in the school or be given a responsibility or a job to do.

* Have in mind the thing you want to do when you leave school. This may be helpful for you to know why it's important to stay in school.

## What Are The Difficulties...

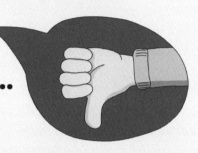

"Teachers picking on me to answer a question when my hand isn't up. It makes me worried and I freeze."
—JOEL, 13

"People being annoying."
—COBY, 13

"Teachers being in my personal space while I'm working, checking up on me and my work."
—WILLIAM, 12

"My brain daydreams about other things like our dogs and sometimes it can waste half the lesson."
—FERN, 12

"Concentrating and getting work done."
—EOGHAN, 12

## "Being shouted at for not listening."

—DONNY, 13

# What Would Help...

"Be clear and give me extra time."—JACK, 15

"I need somewhere safe to retreat to when things become too much."
—DORIAN RAY, 16

"Clear instructions and reminders."—MATT, 15

"I need motivation and someone who understands me."—ASHLEIGH, 13

"Doing activities rather than just listening."—WOODY, 12

"Lending me equipment because I forget."
—ZIYAAD, 15

# Why These Things Help...

"Everyone deserves to be understood."—DAVE, 13

"If the teachers give me reminders, I will remember what equipment to get out."
—DANIEL, 18

"If you give me more time, you will see my true ability."
—JACK, 15

"If I use ear defenders it helps me focus and takes my mind off the noise."—MAX, 12

"If teachers give me what I need, it is an acceptance of who I am."
—CALLUM, 19

"A quieter classroom means I can focus."
—GRACE, 12

# Avoid, Avoid, Avoid...

"Asking me why I don't understand—I don't have an answer for that as I have usually missed something or misunderstood."
—DAISY, 17

"Don't talk to me when I am working because it takes me out of concentration and it's hard to get back in."
—FERN, 12

"Punishing me for things I can't control."
—LEON, 15

"Giving me detentions."
—COBY, 13

"Getting too angry as it makes me nervous and ruins my concentration."
—EOGHAN, 12

# "Saying lots of things at once and saying things too quickly."
—ASHLEIGH, 13

# CHAPTER SIX

# HOMEWORK

**An ADHD brain needs motivation and stimulation.** Unless homework is interesting, purposeful and there seems to be a point to it, you will not be inclined to dedicate time to it.

This causes friction at home and you may get into trouble at school.

This doesn't mean you don't realise that it needs to be done—you just may not have the desire or inclination to actually do it. The trouble is how to marry up getting it done with your disinclination to make it happen.

# Quick Wins

* Let school know you're having trouble getting stuff done and maybe you need shorter or multiple deadlines.

* Make sure the homework is realistic for you to complete on your own (your parent shouldn't be teaching you).

* Make sure the homework is written down correctly—maybe an adult at school can support you with this.

* Use a planner at home so you have an agreed time to do homework. Give yourself a reward afterwards.

* Set up an area at home with as few distractions as possible.

* Eat a protein snack before you tackle homework.

* Break up a big project into smaller steps.

* Do homework at school if you can.

# This is what teenagers said about homework...

## What Are The Difficulties...

"Work should only be done at school. I struggle to focus and revise."—JACK, 15

"Getting myself to do it! Remembering I have homework. Keep my mind from drifting away to other things."—DONNY, 13

"I find it hard to concentrate."—COBY, 13

"Trying to memorise things I'm not interested in."—GRACE, 12

"I struggle to do school work at home because school and home are two separate places in my mind."
—WILLIAM, 12

## "Organisation, remembering things that aren't written down."

—JOEL, 13

# What Would Help...

"Homework supervised at school."—RAPHIE, 18

"Fact sheets, work chunked, homework planner with a consistent routine."—MATT, 15

"Making it a bit easier with pictures and having little notes for what words mean."—TAMZIN, 18

"It helps if my mum types while I tell her what to write —it helps me think a lot more easily."—WOODY, 12

"Maybe a recording that I could put headphones on to listen to."—JACK, 15

"Getting less homework." —FERN, 12

# Why These Things Help...

"I find it really difficult to motivate myself and get started. So being in the best mood to get started is the most effective thing. I've got to be interested in what I am doing and in the right mood to do it."—DAISY, 17

"Using a timetable would make me feel relaxed." —EOGHAN, 12

"If I have breaks halfway through it lets me think." —PATRICK, 12

"I don't think I should do homework at home because that's where I do my own thing and relax and chill." —DANIEL, 18

"If I did homework at school, there's not as many distractions."—COBY, 13

"Homework takes too long; I have other things to do at home."—LEON, 15

# Avoid, Avoid, Avoid...

"Don't nag about
doing homework."
—DONNY, 13

"I need to have dinner first.
It helps if I have a treat
at the end of it."
—WOODY, 12

"Overloading me too much."
—HOLLIE, 14

"Giving unclear
instructions, assuming
I'm just being lazy or
stupid or difficult."
—DORIAN RAY, 16

"Blaming, and saying I'm
lazy. It takes me hours and
hours to start an essay then
hours and hours to do it as my
processing is so slow."
—CALLUM, 19

# "Not allowing me to have more flexibility."

—DAISY, 17

# CHAPTER SEVEN

# TIME KEEPING

**Time is a tricky concept for you. It's not about the ability to read a clock.**

It's just your perception of how much time it takes to do a task and misjudging the time it takes to get somewhere or do something. It's losing your sense of time and realising you have stayed too late, taken too long or not left enough time.

This means that you may be late for stuff. Or you find that you are rushing to get things done as the deadline is approaching. Or you put off a task because you think it's going to take ages (when in reality you could get it done in five minutes).

So you may find you have left too little time or over-compensated and you have too much time to spare. This leads to you getting bored or distracted and then you are still late.

This can be frustrating for those around you and make you feel rubbish.

# Quick Wins

✳ Set multiple alarms on your watch or use a device like Alexa.

✳ Ask friends to remind you.

✳ Work backwards from the time you need to be somewhere and make allowances for obstacles that may happen.

✳ Use post-it notes as reminders.

✳ Time yourself doing the boring stuff you hate, so you know in reality how long it will actually take next time.

# This is what teenagers said about time keeping...

## What Are The Difficulties...

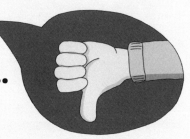

"I am very bad at time keeping; it feels like sometimes every minute is two minutes if it's boring, and time goes really slowly. If the subject is interesting it goes quickly. I find it very hard to tell the time or even know what time of day it is."
—WOODY, 12

"If I get given a due date for an assessment then I will try to get it done on time but if I don't then I will give up and wait till it is late and then I will get it done."
—ASHLEIGH, 13

"Losing track of time so easily."
—FERN, 12

"I always leave things last minute because I can never get myself to do it."
—DONNY, 13

"I have bad anxiety about being late or missing things so it affects my sleep thinking about it."
—MATT, 15

"My attention and concentration can change a lot—sometimes too much so I take too long, and sometimes not being able to focus and settle so I run out of time."
—JOEL, 13

# What Would Help...

"Setting timers for ten minutes rather than saying you have ten minutes."
—GRACE, 12

"I would love for people to be a little more patient with me in terms of time keeping and not to be so judgy, and instead try and help me."
—DAISY, 17

"Having a digital clock watch."—FERN, 12

"Reminders, alarms and timers."—DANIEL, 18

"Having enough time to complete what I need to do."—LEON, 15

"Sometimes a plan sheet with times of what I have to do."
—TAMZIN, 18

# Why These Things Help...

"A timetable can help me remember what time I have to do stuff."—DONNY, 13

"I tend to be forgetful so reminders would help me remember."—EOGHAN, 12

"A timetable would make life easier."—GRACE, 12

"I wouldn't panic about not having enough time if I had reminders."—LEON, 15

"Seeing the time physically count down would help."
—JACK, 15

"I need reminders and alarms so I know what time to do certain things and for how long."—DANIEL, 18

55

# Avoid, Avoid, Avoid...

"Don't be rude or patronising. Be understanding and try and help understand why I actually am late."
—DAISY, 17

"Rushing me."
—MAX, 12

"Yelling about being late."
—ZIYAAD, 15

"Hurrying me up when I'm getting ready as it makes me more stressed, and criticising my mess."
—WILLIAM, 12

"Don't keep telling me."
—DANIEL, 18

# "Don't make a show of it when I'm late."

—DORIAN RAY, 16

# CHAPTER EIGHT

# ORGANISATION

**If your brain is buzzing and you have a zillion things running through your head, you are likely not paying attention to where things ought to go.**

You may chuck your stuff down without thinking, then can't find it when it's time to leave (and you may be running late...).

Or you cannot organise your school work and feel overwhelmed by the volume of notes, revision plans, essays and homework that you need to be on top of. And you don't know where to start with organising it all.

Your bedroom may be a tip. This may be because tidiness doesn't matter to you. You are not interested or motivated to keep things in order, and then the task becomes too big to do anything about it.

# Quick Wins

* Buy boxes, files, hooks, shelves and, most important of all, a label maker so all your stuff has a place to live.

* Make lists and prioritise what needs to be done first.

* Find an app you really like to use to help you organise your life.

* Use a whiteboard, journals and post-its.

* Stick to a routine.

* Make a boring task fun by making it into a game, like timing yourself and beating your score.

* Get rid of clutter or stuff you don't need. Donate it or sell it.

## What Are The Difficulties...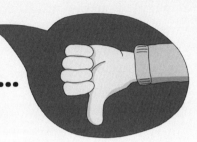

"My organisation is terrible because I go from other stuff to other stuff and don't finish or clear up. I forget everything and always lose my PE kit."—WOODY, 12

"Can't stay organised —my mother still keeps me organised." —RAPHIE, 18

"Remembering where I put stuff, dumping things randomly without thinking of retrieving them or where I'd find them."—DONNY, 13

"If I've had a bad week there are clothes all over my floor, plates and cups in my room. And this disgusts me but sometimes I cannot bring myself to sort it all out, it's overwhelming." —DAISY, 17

"I don't organise my school bag."—JACK, 15

## "Remembering everything."

—WILLIAM, 12

# What Would Help...

"Designated places to keep stuff, like always putting my wallet in a certain drawer."
—DONNY, 13

"Some help organising my stuff at home."
—WILLIAM, 12

"Something to remind me to keep everything together."
—EOGHAN, 12

"Reminders on my phone. Someone to sit and help me organise things."
—MATT, 15

"People not moving things when I have already put something somewhere as I don't want it to be moved out of its spot."
—ASHLEIGH, 13

# "A list of things I need."

—HOLLIE, 14

# Why These Things Help...

"Reminders on my phone take the responsibility away from me to remember." —MATT, 15

"If I used a device like an iPad it would be good because I'm scared of forgetting something in case I get into trouble or am shamed in front of the class." —JACK, 15

"Organising my stuff makes me less stressed because I know I have what I need." —WILLIAM, 12

"I wouldn't be expected to remember things if I had a list." —HOLLIE, 14

"A planner would help me a bit more to know what I need to have done by certain times." —TAMZIN, 18

"Lists and prompts would remind me and give me a routine to follow." —MAX, 12

# Avoid, Avoid, Avoid...

"Saying that I'm not trying and saying that it is really easy to organise my stuff as it makes me feel upset." —EOGHAN, 12

"Blaming and the use of humiliating, belittling language." —CALLUM, 19

"Nagging." —JACK, 15

"Not giving a written down list of what to do." —TAMZIN, 18

"Do not keep telling me." —DANIEL, 18

"Making me do lots of things at once. Break it down into simple instructions, one at a time." —WOODY, 12

# CHAPTER NINE

# GETTING STUFF DONE

## Sometimes a task is too big and you can't get started.

It may be that you are distracted and not motivated to get a task done.

You are brilliant at putting things off and not getting it done. You procrastinate and nothing gets started.

This is because boring stuff is so dull and not motivating as your brain needs a constant shot of dopamine.

Or it may be that you want something to be perfect and this is putting you off getting started, as you fear the task won't turn out exactly right.

Then of course, the task doesn't get done which may be making you feel uneasy.

# Quick Wins

* Break down tasks into small steps and tackle each one at a time.

* Give yourself a reward or a purpose to complete the task.

* Make a playlist or listen to an audio book while you get the boring thing done.

* Make the task fun and introduce silliness or competition.

* Diarise the task so you feel prepared.

* Get a buddy to do the task with you so it is not boring.

* If you are trying to study, then have a video buddy working alongside or agree to check in with each other at a certain time.

# This is what teenagers said about getting stuff done...

## What Are The Difficulties...

"If I'm not interested I struggle to motivate myself."
—MATT, 15

"I can do special interest things but apart from that it's hard."—RAPHIE, 18

"Wanting to do it when it's not interesting."—PATRICK, 12

"School work is hard to get done, mainly classes I don't like and household chores."—GRACE, 12

"Hard to start but once started I am okay."—DAVE, 13

## "Just doing it in the first place."

—EOGHAN, 12

# What Would Help...

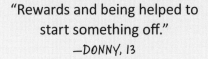

"Rewards and being helped to start something off."
—DONNY, 13

"Tick list or reminders."
—LEON, 15

"A reason or reward to get me into it."—JOEL, 13

"Giving me work that feels purposeful, or on a topic I'm actually interested in."
—DORIAN RAY, 16

"Make them more fun."
—TAMZIN, 18

"Music helps a lot."
—DAVE, 13

# Why These Things Help...

"I think seeing things that need doing reminds me to do them."—DAISY, 17

"If I lose focus, a tick list helps me to find where I'm up to."
—MATT, 15

"If I am reminded, I can stay on track."
—PATRICK, 12

"Getting a reward would give me an incentive."
—WILLIAM, 12

"If it's fun, there's a better chance of doing things."
—TAMZIN, 18

"If it was purposeful and meaningful, it would give me the motivation to actually do the work."
—DORIAN RAY, 16

# Avoid, Avoid, Avoid...

"Adults should avoid nagging me to do things; it only makes me want to resist them."
—DAISY, 17

"Getting cross when I need it explained again."
—MATT, 15

"Getting impatient as it makes me feel like I am in trouble which makes me feel stressed."
—EOGHAN, 12

"Blaming—instead offer me support."
—CALLUM, 19

"Shouting and using a disapproving tone if I've forgotten something or not started what I should have."
—JOEL, 13

# "Giving me too many things at once."

—LEON, 15

# CHAPTER TEN

# FAMILY

**Being in a family can be tricky.**

Your natural teenage hormones are shrieking for you to be alone, retreat into your room and find comfort in finding your tribe.

But there are still pressures to be with the family. Mealtimes, travelling in the car, special occasions, holidays, day trips.

You may have siblings who get on your nerves and there are arguments and fights because you clash. You may be jealous or feel hateful. Grandparents or cousins may be on your case and tut-tut which you hate.

You may feel like your family members treat you and your siblings differently and that you cause too much trouble. This makes you feel sad and lonely. This may result in you being rude and saying unkind things that you don't really mean.

All these feelings are okay. But it is a good plan to work out ways to live together peacefully which will mean educating everyone about ADHD.

# Quick Wins

* Educate your family— share this book with them.

* Ask family members to have reasonable expectations of what you can manage.

* Remove yourself from a situation if you're getting wound up.

* Explain to family how you are feeling and what they can do to help you.

* Use your voice to let your family know, politely, what you need.

* Encourage your family to celebrate your successes.

* Find ways to have fun together with your family, doing stuff you like.

## What Are The Difficulties...

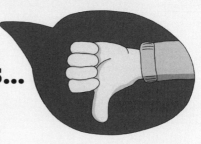

"Sometimes I don't get along with my sister."—GRACE, 12

"Getting into arguments with my siblings and parents."—EOGHAN, 12

"My little sister and doing things when my parents tell me to, especially when I don't want to."—ASHLEIGH, 13

"My younger brother winding me up; he knows how to push my buttons which really frustrates me and often gets me into a lot of trouble."—WILLIAM, 12

"Not everyone in my family knows that I can't control my brain."—TAMZIN, 18

## "Getting angry and taking it out on my sister when I don't mean to."

—FERN, 12

# What Would Help...

"If my brother didn't annoy me and if I wasn't so reactive."
—MATT, 15

"Having a bit of me time with all the family so I can explain what I'm feeling."
—FERN, 12

"If sometimes people were nicer."
—PATRICK, 12

"Sometimes splitting us up, so me and my brother can each get what we need from our mum and dad."
—JOEL, 13

"For my parents to make it clear in their actions that they're on my side."
—DORIAN RAY, 16

# "Maybe for my parents to have a little more patience."
—JACK, 15

# Why These Things Help...

"Splitting me and my brother up would allow us to calm down and think about what we did before coming up with a plan for next time."
—WILLIAM, 12

"If they understood me more, it would avoid arguments as they will know what frustrates me and makes me anxious."
—EOGHAN, 12

"I'd feel more obliged to meet them halfway if they were being nice to me."—DONNY, 13

"Sometimes I need space and understanding."
—JOEL, 13

"My family would be happier and there would be fewer arguments."—MATT, 15

# Avoid, Avoid, Avoid...

"Confronting me when I'm angry. Telling me off in the moment."
—MATT, 15

"Big and unreasonable punishments especially for my impulsive behaviour."
—WILLIAM, 12

"Don't shout."
—DONNY, 13

"Asking too much of me when I am overwhelmed."
—JOEL, 13

"Telling off when there's not a real reason."
—TAMZIN, 18

"Hugging and touching me."
—DANIEL, 18

# CHAPTER ELEVEN

# EMOTIONS

**Think of your emotions pouring into a bucket.**
That bucket gets full really quickly for people with ADHD.

This means that you feel things MASSIVELY.

So you get jealous, angry, weepy, worried, scared, excited, silly to an extreme level very quickly.

You then may get stuck in this emotion and need help to move on. Your bucket needs emptying.

You may be particularly sensitive and often you are incredibly perceptive of other people's emotions and how they are feeling.

Sometimes you get so angry no one is listening that you kick off and are rude and aggressive. You then want to drop it quickly but the adults keep bringing up your rudeness and piling on the punishments. This just makes you more angry.

Sometimes you tell lies just to get them off your back. Or you lie because you're being questioned about something and you really can't remember. Or you just want to make it sound more exciting because you have a creative brain. Then everything escalates and they're focusing so much on the lie. This makes you furious.

Add in that your teenage hormones are kicking off big time, which may explain why your emotions are all over the place. You may be experiencing feelings that are alien to you. You are also thinking more about sex and your own sexuality.

All of these feelings are **normal**. However, if you feel you need to speak to a professional, there are contacts at the back of this book.

# Quick Wins

* Explain to people how you are feeling.

* Sometimes you don't actually need a solution; you just need to find someone to listen to you.

* Have your own plan in place for what you can do to feel better; some ideas could be meditation, mindfulness, running, singing, art, hitting a cushion, drinking water, having a bath, a hug, a massage.

* Let people know what you would like them to do to help you.

* You may need some time alone before you can engage with anyone.

* Let people know that you like to feel some sense of control—so instead of being told what to do, you'd prefer to be given opportunities to work it out yourself or be given choices.

# This is what teenagers said about emotions...

## What Are The Difficulties...

"Overthinking, anxiety, fear of missing out (FOMO) and I get angry."—LEXI, 12

"I can go from one extreme to another. When I get overwhelmed I can either shout or cry. Sometimes the same situation will have a different response from me."
—GRACE, 12

"I get upset, let things annoy me, I'm sensitive."
—JACK, 15

"I get very upset by criticism, disapproval or negative tones and shouting."
—JOEL, 13

"Anger over situations that I shouldn't be angry over. Over competitive, too critical of people."
—DAVE, 13

## "Anger and sadness."
—ZIYAAD, 15

74

# What Would Help...

"Dance, and touching silk material."—LEXI, 12

"Being able to calm down before things escalate."
—DAISY, 17

"To maybe go outside at school and have some alone time at home."—FERN, 12

"Not to go to crowded places."—DANIEL, 18

"My dog and rabbits."
—MAX, 12

"Less blame and recognition of effort."
—RAPHIE, 18

# Why These Things Help...

"Dance helps my anger and I release everything out on it and put my love into it. It helps with my hyperactivity as I can get my energy out."
—LEXI, 12

"If someone comforted me, it would help me as I would feel safe and that someone can relate to me."—EOGHAN, 12

"Talking about my emotions would make me learn that you can cry."—PATRICK, 12

"People that understand me would bring me back down to a good place."—DAVE, 13

"Allowing me calm time gives me processing time and I'm not in fight mode."—MATT, 15

"I can take in what they're saying better if I'm not feeling attacked."—JOEL, 13

75

# Avoid, Avoid, Avoid...

"Forcing apologies. Assuming that because I'm not crying or emotional that I'm not sorry. I often am but I just can't show it or say it."
—MATT, 15

"Don't make me feel like my feelings do not matter."
—DORIAN RAY, 16

"Yelling."
—TAMZIN, 18

"Being over-reactive and shouting."
—WILLIAM, 12

"Punishing me doesn't help me; I don't learn from it especially when I can't help something."
—LEXI, 12

# "Don't talk to me when I am angry."

—DAVE, 13

# CHAPTER TWELVE

# RISKY BEHAVIOUR

**An ADHD brain thrives on stimulation.** The brain is craving the missing neurotransmitters we spoke about in Chapter One.

Risky behaviour creates that dopamine rush that an ADHD brain is seeking and craving.

Add in your impulsivity, and you can see how sometimes you put yourself in risky or dangerous situations. You are not stopping to think if something is a good idea; you just go for it.

But some of this stuff can get you into trouble. With your friends, with your parents, with school and with the police. Many young people with ADHD end up in the criminal justice system. It is estimated that 25% of people in prison have ADHD (this figure may be even higher if we take account of undiagnosed people in the system).[5]

If you are smoking weed or vaping, studies show that this may also be affecting brain development. Which is not helpful to a brain already struggling with neurotransmitter chemistry.[6,7]

**So be careful. Be wise.**

# Quick Wins

* Choose carefully the people you hang around with, as they may encourage you to try risky stuff which could be dangerous or illegal.

* Let your friends know to support you if you want to say no to drugs or sex.

* Practise some things to say to your friends to get you out of a risky situation. Things like "Vapes give me a rash", "I've got to go as we're getting a takeaway".

* Go for risky activities that are more controlled like parkour, mountain biking, skateboarding or wall climbing.

* Don't alienate your parents. They will naturally want to protect you and tell you not to get involved in any risky behaviour. But they are on your side (even if it doesn't feel like it) and they will help you if you find yourself with a massive problem. Keep talking to them.

# This is what teenagers said about risky behaviour...

## What Are The Difficulties...

"If I like the look of it, I'll do it."
—DAVE, 13

"When I am really excited or angry I do not think rationally."
—DAISY, 17

"Social media and online stuff could be risky."
—DANIEL, 18

"Drinking alcohol."
—CALLUM, 19

"Running away up the road to the park when my emotions are in overdrive."
—WILLIAM, 12

## "Sometimes I jump in without thinking."

—TAMZIN, 18

# What Would Help...

"Being redirected to do something else."—DAISY, 17

"I use music and exercise as much as possible to distract."—RAPHIE, 18

"More understanding and help with consequences of actions, maybe a picture book."—MAX, 12

"People being honest and for people to try and explain everything."—FERN, 12

"Being able to talk about it in advance."—WILLIAM, 12

"Having more self-worth."—DORIAN RAY, 16

# Why These Things Help...

"I need reminding about the dangers because I forget."—DONNY, 13

"Real cause-and-effect style conversations to assess risk prior to certain events so I know what may happen."—MATT, 15

"To be able to understand my actions and try to have a plan for next time."—WILLIAM, 12

"I don't want to get hurt."—HOLLIE, 14

"Thinking about the dangers of what could happen."—DAVE, 13

"Knowing about a risk helps moderate behaviour."—CALLUM, 19

# Avoid, Avoid, Avoid...

"Expecting 'normal' behaviour and not explaining the risks in a down-to-earth way rather than a lecture."
—MATT, 15

"Being overly cross or reactive and chasing after me when I'm in 'flight' mode."
—WILLIAM, 12

"Telling me off too much, because I'm not always in complete control."
—DAISY, 17

"Don't scream at me for doing it."
—DONNY, 13

"Being embarrassed about my behaviour. I need to know the risks with acceptance."
—RAPHIE, 18

# "Shouting and being too restrictive."

—PATRICK, 12

# CHAPTER THIRTEEN

# FRIENDSHIPS

## This can be tough.

Everyone I guess wants to have friends that they can do stuff with, have a laugh and share thoughts and secrets. TV shows and movies set you up to desire the perfect gang of loyal friends.

## But having ADHD means that friendships can be tricky.

You may be unreliable (time management again!), you may blurt out a secret (impulsive), or overshare or be too dramatic.

And you may be embarrassing or told you are too sensitive.

These things can feel hurtful and can make you feel lonely. You may feel rejected and misunderstand other people's intentions. You feel they don't like you, but in reality they do.

You may find school lunchtimes lonely and are being subjected to bullies and unkind remarks.

A good way to make friends is to find people who are like you and have similar interests.

By the way, I do not think attending classes to learn "how to make friends" or "social skills groups" are particularly successful.

Finally, you may have a funny, quirky, spirited personality. Do not change it to fit in.

# Quick Wins

* Find your tribe.

* Find people who are like you, have the same interests and understand you, and really like your quirkiness.

* Try and avoid social media if it is making you unhappy.

* Tell an adult if things are getting too much and you feel lonely.

* Avoid going to groups or activities where you feel uncomfortable.

* Let adults know that you do not want to attend any formal "social skills training" groups.

# This is what teenagers said about friendships...

## What Are The Difficulties...

"Making friends and keeping them."—JACK, 15

"Hurting people's feelings, saying things I thought were funny but might be offensive."—MATT, 15

"I feel like my friends don't like me and want me around. Big groups are hard."—GRACE, 12

"Sometimes I don't watch my words so I can be misunderstood or offend people."
—WILLIAM, 12

"Falling out with people and fighting."
—DAVE, 13

## "Trying too hard to be liked."

—JACK, 15

# What Would Help...

"My friends understanding my ADHD."—EOGHAN, 12

"Friends understanding me."—FERN, 12

"Choosing friends that understand me."—DAVE, 13

"Dance helps me to make friends."—LEXI, 12

"If people see me for who I am. I am really nice and would make a great friend if people didn't make fun of me."—JACK, 15

"Being accepted as a person, not a behaviour."—LEON, 15

# Why These Things Help...

"Friends understanding about ADHD would avoid arguments."—EOGHAN, 12

"I am not good at conversations so I need people to understand."—TAMZIN, 18

"I would feel like everyone else does if I had good friends."—JACK, 15

"A good friend will support me through the good times and bad and stick up for me and help me."—DAVE, 13

"If there was education about hidden disabilities it would save me a lot of grief."—DORIAN RAY, 16

"Friends knowing about ADHD would help explain my impulsive words and actions."—WILLIAM, 12

# Avoid, Avoid, Avoid...

"Assuming I'm a bad person."
—LEON, 15

"If I report bullying don't ignore me."—LEXI, 12

"Always asking about my friends."—PATRICK, 12

"Trying to control who I can and can't be friends with."
—DAVE, 13

"Not allowing me to explain and ruining the chance to repair the friendship."
—WILLIAM, 12

# "Don't get involved in my friendships."

—DONNY, 13

# CHAPTER FOURTEEN

# FOOD

## Food may be an issue for a few reasons.

First, eating a meal involves social constraints. Sitting at a table. Forced conversation. Sitting still. Waiting. Noisy. All a bit too much for you if you have ADHD.

Then the actual textures and smells may be off-putting. Trying new foods may be a huge hurdle.

You may be on medication which may affect your appetite.

If you feel that food is connected to the way you look and this is causing you distress, please speak to an adult who may be able to help. There are contact details at the back of this book.

We know social media can cause many teenagers to feel negatively about their bodies. If you are following any accounts that make you feel sad, less worthy or are encouraging you to do anything unsafe, immediately unfollow and talk to an adult.

# Quick Wins

* Try to include protein into your diet. Starting off the day with protein is a really good idea as it will help you with focus.

* Avoid sugar which will give you a huge rush of energy, but then very quickly you will crash and feel lethargic and sleepy.

* Try to keep busy if you find you're snacking on anything unhealthy.

* Take supplements of Omega 3 which are recommended to help with focus.[8]

* Instead of your meal piled onto one plate, select what you want to eat from small dishes on the table.

* If you go to a restaurant, choose one where you can get up, move and select from a buffet.

## What Are The Difficulties...

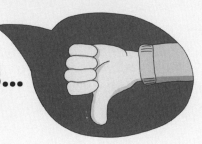

"I am motivated by the comfort of food which can get out of control."
—JOEL, 13

"I am obsessed with eating healthily—we can't have sugar in the house as I have no off switch."
—CALLUM, 19

"I do not recognise when I am full. If food is in front of me I just want to eat it and am not very good at limiting myself."
—GRACE, 12

"Meds affect my appetite."
—RAPHIE, 18

"Making a decision on what to have for my meals."
—DANIEL, 18

"Not eating enough, particularly in the morning."
—DAVE, 13

# What Would Help...

"If I feel like snacking on sugar, having something to chew like chewing gum." —EOGHAN, 12

"It would help knowing what nutrients and ingredients are in the food."—WILLIAM, 12

"Having healthier foods around."—JOEL, 13

"Have a list of what I like." —TAMZIN, 18

"Giving me choices." —DANIEL, 18

"Finding something else to do." —FERN, 12

# Why These Things Help...

"I need things to do because I snack when I'm bored." —FERN, 12

"Chewing gum would satisfy the sensory part of me that wants to chew."—EOGHAN, 12

"If food was restricted that would provide me with the filter I need."—GRACE, 12

"If I had a healthy snack it would stop me from stealing food when I know that I am not supposed to be eating." —ASHLEIGH, 13

"I think good role models, as I learn from other people a lot." —DAISY, 17

"If I ate when I was hungry rather than at dinner time, I could get calories as I haven't eaten all day because of my meds."—MATT, 15

# Avoid, Avoid, Avoid...

"Don't shout. Rather actually find a way to help."
—DONNY, 13

"Commenting on what I eat and judging my habits."
—DAISY, 17

"Don't try to force me to try new things or eat things I don't like, or take me to restaurants, or look disapprovingly at me when I can't finish."
—DORIAN RAY, 16

"Embarrassing me, judging me, giving me the wrong food as a comfort."
—JOEL, 13

"Avoid giving me sugary food."
—RAPHIE, 18

## "Forcing me to eat."
—EOGHAN, 12

# CHAPTER FIFTEEN

# SLEEP

**Scientists will tell you that teenagers need about 9 to 10 hours of sleep a night to function well the next day. Your body and brain are developing and sleep is needed for good developmental growth.[9]**

## But I bet you are not getting anything like this.

Switching off a busy ADHD brain can be really tricky. Those pesky thoughts, opinions, ideas that are buzzing around your head are challenging your sleepy cells to switch off.

You may be thinking about the task you procrastinated about and didn't get done. Or about the impulsive thing you did that got you into trouble.

Plus being in bed is actually boring. Your brain would much rather be doing something fun and exciting.

You also may have "restless legs" where you feel an overwhelming urge to move your legs and may get an itchy feeling. Some people say it feels like ants crawling on their legs.

Then you find it almost impossible to get up in the morning; you're being screamed at that you're going to be late, but you are exhausted from so little sleep.

# Quick Wins

* Switch off your mobile phone an hour before sleep and charge it downstairs so you're not tempted to have a peep at social media.

* You may like complete darkness or low-level lighting.

* You might need your room to be cool or you may like a weighted blanket.

* Experiment with different alarms or your own playlist to wake you up and decide whether you like the curtains open or the light on.

* Have a journal by your bed to dump any thoughts or things you need to do.

* Set up your own bedtime routine to calm your brain.

* Buy alternative gadgets to a phone, such as an alarm clock, radio, Alexa for audio books etc.—nothing that connects you to the apps and games you find distracting.

* Find out what switches off your thoughts. It could be listening to calm music, white noise, ASMR sounds or an audio book. Maybe an aromatherapy diffuser or watching a lava lamp.

* Avoid heavy conversations or watching anything disturbing too close to bed.

# This is what teenagers said about sleep...

## What Are The Difficulties...

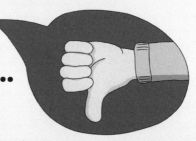

"I can't fall asleep and can't wake up."—ZIYAAD, 15

"Sometimes I go to bed late and fall asleep quite late so I fall behind on sleep which affects my day."—DONNY, 13

"Getting too hyper before sleep."
—EOGHAN, 12

"I don't like being on my own. Waking in the night and not being able to get back to sleep by myself."—GRACE, 12

"Getting to sleep and staying asleep and also getting up very early in the morning."—ASHLEIGH, 13

## "I struggle to fall asleep and then I struggle to wake up."

—MATT, 15

# What Would Help...

"I listen to relaxing sounds at night."—JACK, 15

"Switching gadgets off earlier."—LEON, 15

"Good routines and ways to wind down."—MATT, 15

"I listen to Headspace and use a canopy and weighted blanket."—RAPHIE, 18

"To put the phone in another room when I'm going to sleep."—JOEL, 13

"A strict sleep routine and reading to me helps. I have four blankets, a duvet and a weighted blanket. I sleep with a woolly hat on with a mask and my favourite teddies which all help me feel secure." —DAVE, 13

# Why These Things Help...

"Listening to meditative music helps relax my mind and I feel safe."—GRACE, 12

"Routines help my brain switch off."—MATT, 15

"Sleep aids like essential oils, sleep stories would calm me down to sleep."—WILLIAM, 12

"If I fall asleep with Glee playing it fills my head with good thoughts." —LEXI, 12

"My weighted blanket feels nice to me." —TAMZIN, 18

"I need to feel relaxed to sleep." —JACK, 15

# Avoid, Avoid, Avoid...

"Never talk about bad stuff at night or argue and shout."
—LEXI, 12

"Making me go to bed when I am not tired."
—DANIEL, 18

"Don't guilt me about sleeping late."
—DORIAN RAY, 16

"Shouting and being impatient."
—GRACE, 12

"Let me wake up in my own time and so don't open the curtains."
—PATRICK, 12

## "Saying 'just go back to sleep' and leaving the room."

—WILLIAM, 12

# CHAPTER SIXTEEN

# SCREENS

**The genie is out of the bottle. We are living in the 21st century and technology dominates all our lives.**

It's very tempting to be on a screen all day. A screen provides your brain with the stuff it is craving. Constant eye movement, problem solving, connection with friends, as well as a massive dopamine hit. Game designers deliberately make games compelling and addictive, so that when you reach the end of a level, it is sooooooooo tempting to just continue to play.

You may also be on a screen as you are bored and it is a quick fix.

But this may affect your sleep and your relationships in the family. I bet you've been nagged today about how long you're on a screen. You also may be missing out on other opportunities to have fun and meet real people.

We also know there are potential dangers when you are online. There are unscrupulous people who will target teenagers, encouraging you to do things that you are uncomfortable with or which put you at risk, whether that is exposing yourself sexually, saying unkind things you wouldn't normally in real life or being encouraged to harm yourself or others in any way.

Remember your impulsive, risk-seeking brain—be mindful that it is okay to say no, delete a "friend" and leave or unfollow.

# Quick Wins

* Decide with your parents how long you feel is reasonable to be on a screen.

* Write in a planner when you will be on a screen and what is happening after (has to be something motivating for you).

* Have an audible alarm so you know when it is time to do something else which is fun and stimulating.

* See if your parent would like to join you in a game or activity online so they can understand what you are doing.

* Agree that an adult in your family will quickly check your device periodically to make sure you are keeping yourself safe.

## What Are The Difficulties...

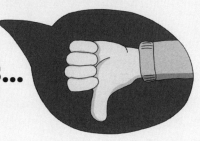

"Arguments on Snapchat or WhatsApp or watching my friends be together without me on TikTok."
—LEXI, 12

"I get obsessed with games and can spend hours on them."—MATT, 15

"I've got into trouble for things that I've been sent and forwarded on."—DAVE, 13

"I can waste a lot of time looking at things when I've got other things I should be doing."
—JOEL, 13

"Can't come off and have no sense of time."—CALLUM, 19

## "Using a screen when I'm very bored or upset and it distracts me."

—DAISY, 17

# What Would Help...

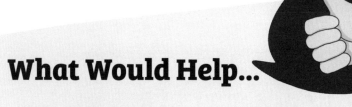

"Having more stimulating things to do."—DAISY, 17

"Going outside and doing other things to distract you."—DAVE, 13

"Ten-minute warning before I get off."—EOGHAN, 12

"Parents saying I can do something fun or active when I come off."—WILLIAM, 12

"Setting an alarm to switch my devices off."—LEON, 15

"Having reminders to take breaks and knowing it's okay to come away even if I haven't won. Also I need a countdown."—MATT, 15

## "Try to not reply to an argument on text or reply when I am emotional."

—LEXI, 12

# Why These Things Help...

"I enjoy spending time with my family so doing something with them after screen time would be an incentive."
—WILLIAM, 12

"Finding something productive to do would take me away from my screen."
—FERN, 12

"Going outside gives you a break from them."—DAVE, 13

"Using warnings would help me remember when I need to finish and not start something new."—EOGHAN, 12

"Everyone reads texts differently—it is so much better to talk it through."
—LEXI, 12

# "If I used a timer I would realise how long I have been on and can come off."

—GRACE, 12

# Avoid, Avoid, Avoid...

"Switching off the internet. Screaming at me to come off mid-game."
—MATT, 15

"Leaving me for a long time without checking that I haven't lost track of time."
—JOEL, 13

"Snatching the iPad off me before I'm done or stressing me out over the time I've spent on the screen."
—WILLIAM, 12

"Reminding me that I should be out with my friends only aggravates me."—DAISY, 17

"Taking screens away without giving me a warning."
—FERN, 12

## "Switching my Xbox off when I am doing something."

—DANIEL, 18

CHAPTER SEVENTEEN

# MONEY

**An ADHD brain craves excitement and stimulation.** Spending money and buying a shiny new object can give you a quick dopamine hit that gives you immediate pleasure.

But this can be problematic for you as too often you buy the thing, use the thing for two minutes, then get bored and want the next thing. Sound familiar?

You may find it difficult to save as any money burns a hole in your pocket because you are impulsive. Then you have no money for the things you really need.

You may also find that you have a good idea or want to take up a new activity. So you research like crazy, spend your money, start the project or activity, then get quickly bored and discard it or quit. Money wasted.

You also may not be able to keep track of your spending and may be tempted to get a credit card but then end up in debt or with bills to pay.

# Quick Wins

* Decide what you want to spend your money on and print out a picture so it's visual.

* Stick the picture up on a wall and tally how much you are saving so you can instantly see how much you need to continue to save.

* Negotiate with your parents for you to do chores to earn extra money.

* Use apps on your phone to show what you are spending and saving.

* Use a banking prepaid card.

* Check your bank balance at a regular time to help you manage your money. You could set an alarm to remind you.

# This is what teenagers said about money...

## What Are The Difficulties...

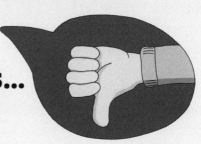

"Obsessively saving because I have a fear of spending too much."—DAISY, 17

"Spending it too quick."—DONNY, 13

"I can't save. If I see something I like I just want to buy it."—GRACE, 12

"I spend it as soon as I get it."
—MATT, 15

"I have no idea what's in my bank account."
—CALLUM, 19

## "I struggle to manage money—if I have it I want things."

—RAPHIE, 18

# What Would Help...

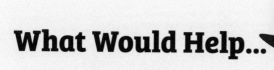

"I will take a photo of something I want to buy and then think about it for a week or two. If after that time I still want it, I can get it."—GRACE, 12

"Having a budget only once a week."—ASHLEIGH, 13

"A plan to budget my money."—DANIEL, 18

"Learning and knowing how best to manage my money."—WILLIAM, 12

"To try and start saving up."—FERN, 12

## "Learning about how money works in the outside world instead of just school."

—TAMZIN, 18

# Why These Things Help...

"Having an amount to spend so you can't go over a limit and spend it all at once."
—DONNY, 13

"When you know that you have a budget you know you can only spend that amount in that week."—ASHLEIGH, 13

"I want to learn about money, avoid getting into debt and understand the risks."
—WILLIAM, 12

"So I know how much to spend and leave enough for my bills and gym."—DANIEL, 18

"At school I didn't learn about taxes or stuff like that; I just learnt counting money."
—TAMZIN, 18

"If I saved, I would have more money to spend on nice things, not just sweets."
—DAVE, 13

# Avoid, Avoid, Avoid...

"Giving me a lot of money all at once."—FERN, 12

"Recommending stuff I should buy which I don't need or want."—WILLIAM, 12

"Letting me just spend it, maybe if I had to wait I might change my mind on what I want."—MATT, 15

"Giving unlimited money without teaching us about it."
—TAMZIN, 18

"Just giving us more money—we don't learn to manage it."
—RAPHIE, 18

"Giving money but not helping me save."
—DAVE, 13

# CHAPTER EIGHTEEN

# HYGIENE

Keeping clean and hygienic is obviously important. No one wants to sit next to someone who stinks or looks grubby.

**You know this. But still you may find keeping clean a challenge.**

This may be because keeping hygienic is dull. You'd rather be on a screen or talking to your friends than having a bath.

Brushing teeth for a whole minute is boring and the toothbrush hurts your gums.

Standing under a shower is repetitive and means getting wet, cold and uncomfortable.

The pressure of the water may be painful.

Washing hair may actually hurt and the smell of the shampoo may be unbearable.

Towels are rough and scratchy.

But if you don't keep up a hygienic routine, particularly if you've played sport or are on your period, then you may get people noticing that you smell, or your teeth and gums get sore and your breath smells.

# Quick Wins

QUICK WINS

* Stick to a daily routine—put it in a planner. Decide if you'd like a bath, shower or to use wipes.

* Use a timer in the bathroom.

* Make a playlist to motivate you.

* Have comfy clothes ready to put on straight away.

* Use really, really soft towels.

* Use toiletries that are unperfumed or have a smell you love.

* Use a specialist toothbrush that won't aggravate your gums and toothpaste that tastes okay.

* Reward yourself if you keep to a routine.

# This is what teenagers said about hygiene...

## What Are The Difficulties...

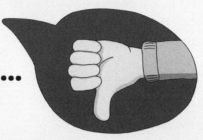

"It is hard to wash my hair." —FERN, 12

"When I'm grumpy I don't wanna do anything at all. I want to sleep and not talk so anything requiring energy feels exhausting." —DAISY, 17

"I can forget to brush my teeth and I take too long in the shower." —LEXI, 12

"Remembering to brush my teeth." —LEON, 15

"Remembering to have a shower or wash and brush my hair." —WILLIAM, 12

"I can't be bothered to wash." —JOEL, 13

# What Would Help...

"Set time aside for mum to help me wash my hair."
—FERN, 12

"Someone monitoring me to remind me to do it."
—EOGHAN, 12

"Making it a definite 'to do' thing in my routine."—JOEL, 13

"Routines are very good; my mum lets me check the smell of shower gel to see if I like it."—MATT, 15

"Reminders to brush or reminders to get out the shower."—LEXI, 12

# "Visual reminders of what to do and when."

—WILLIAM, 12

# Why These Things Help...

"A reminder would help me remember to wash."
—EOGHAN, 12

"A routine gives me control."
—MATT, 15

"Getting into a routine will get me into good habits."
—WILLIAM, 12

"If I had a routine it would stop me being criticised by my family."—JOEL, 13

"It would make me feel better about myself in body and mind."—DORIAN RAY, 16

# "If I had six showers a week I would smell really nice."

—PATRICK, 12

# Avoid, Avoid, Avoid...

"Forcing me—it has to be on my terms. If I miss my morning shower (if I sleep in) then I can't just have it another time; I have to prepare my mind to do it later in the day."—MATT, 15

"Nagging me over and over."
—DANIEL, 18

"Constantly reminding me. I am almost an adult and will always do things eventually and will face the consequences if I don't."
—DAISY, 17

"Constantly reminding me to shower."—WILLIAM, 12

"Shouting."—LEON, 15

# "Dictating when I wash. Instead give me a plan and reminders."

—RAPHIE, 18

# CHAPTER NINETEEN

# THE LAST WORD GOES TO...

I think for people with ADHD and their families, speaking to others is so so important.
—Daisy, 17

Adults to lay off us a bit and others need to understand us more so they can help us.
—Donny, 13

Know you're not alone and there are others who can relate to how you feel. It's not all bad as there are positives to having ADHD.
—William, 12

Having supportive parents has been great. They don't let me get away with bad behaviour but they changed how they parent me to help my ADHD. I was diagnosed late and I thought I was bad but my mum has always told me my brain worked differently than others. She has always made changes around me to help me.
—Matt, 15

You can tell your parents anything and you probably won't get in trouble.
—Fern, 12

More ADHD understanding in school including social groups, mentors and celebration of ADHD as a positive.
—Joel, 13

Be yourself, don't let people tell you who can't be; don't listen to people if they're putting you down, prove them wrong; try not to get in conflict with people. Have a good relationship with your mum and dad and always be open and honest.
—Dave, 13

# CHAPTER TWENTY

# YOU ARE AWESOME

# You see the world differently which can be amazing.

# You need some help to get things done.

# The adults should listen to you when you tell them what you need.

**You need kindness and understanding.**

**You have ADHD and YOU are awesome.**

**Use your voice. It matters. YOU matter.**

# Juicy Bonus

I have produced a pack of ten templates to help you:

* Saving Money

* Meal Planner

* Information for Teachers
  and Club Leaders

* Weekly Planner

* Revision Planner

* Feelings Check-In

* What to Do When
  I Am Upset

* What to Say to Me

* New Medication Diary

* Getting It Done Planner

**Your parents or any other adults
can download them for free at
www.adhdteensurvivalguide.com**

# Info for Parents

When my son was diagnosed with ADHD back in 1996 there was no information available that really helped our family. There was no internet, support groups or conversations about the condition.

I felt I was a terrible parent, made tons of mistakes and we got so much wrong. There was no help or guidance. It was lonely.

But now things are sooooooo different for you and your family.

There are well-known people who talk about their diagnosis. There are ADHD support groups online and in real life. There is help and understanding. Yay!

We are having the conversation. Which is brilliant.

We must encourage our teenagers to use their voice. They know what they need. We must listen to them.

Finally, if you'd like more support, ADHD learning and a bucket full of love, check out our **Together Stronger Club**. This is an online membership for parents to provide more understanding about ADHD and how best to support your teenager at home and school.

# TOGETHER STRONGER Club

**Benefits for members:**

* Complimentary consultation with Soli (me)

* Weekly live coaching sessions

* ADHD training videos

* Interviews with experts

* Free resources

* Meet-up group in real life

**Join us: www.togetherstronger.club**

# Afterword for Parents

The teenager with ADHD is at risk. The odds are that he or she will have lived a life that has had a soundtrack of repeated adult irritability and criticism. They are likely to respond impatiently or angrily to instructions or advice, however well-meant. They will not find it easy to provide feedback to parents, teachers or friends on what they can and cannot do; what works for them, and what is really annoying advice.

That means it is hard for others to understand what is difficult for ADHD teenagers. ADHD is itself diverse. Each individual with ADHD is different. They will need to find a way of saying what it is that is particularly difficult for them, what would help, and what there can be too much of. There cannot be a single cookbook on the standard way to support, teach and live with that person.

Except, of course, to listen to what they say. Yet it is not easy for any one person with ADHD to explain just how they are different and what would make sense for them. It gets easier if other teenagers with ADHD can say what works and what does not.

This book makes it possible for a teenager with ADHD (and their parents or teachers) to see what others say and, almost certainly, find something they identify with and say so. That can be a powerful experience for all concerned. Not only because it gets the message across about what might work but because it lifts self-esteem and self -confidence so that they can tackle life positively and rewardingly.

–**Professor Peter Hill,** Consultant Child and Adolescent Psychiatrist

# Info for Teachers

Thank you for reading this book. I hope it has given you some understanding why some pupils may be finding the environment of school really tough.

I taught in London schools for 30 years and met many incredible professionals who were outstanding at their job.

However, I also came across some who were not.

And in my support groups, I hear of situations where teachers are shaming, blaming and punishing teenagers. Detentions will not change the behaviour of a pupil with ADHD. All they will do is make a pupil angry, disaffected and cause barriers to attending school.

Pupils with SEND are five times more likely to be excluded from school. This cannot be right. Our children with ADHD deserve better life chances.[10]

I hope that having read this book, you can see the need to do things differently for pupils with ADHD. Differentiation and reasonable adjustments mean our children are able to attend and can thrive. Do not waste the talents of the extraordinary pupils with ADHD.

You could be that teacher in your school who is the champion of our children.

It is vital that teachers understand about ADHD and know how to make adjustments.

So:

1. Give all your staff a copy of this book.

2. Book my ADHD staff training immediately. Here are my details: www.yellow-sun.com/adhd

**"The training was honestly the best and most relatable training we have ever had! To get all staff engaged and interested is always a tough one but you managed it!"**

**SENCO**
**(Special Educational Needs Coordinator)**

# Extra Useful Stuff

## SCHOOL
### Voice Typing on Google Docs
*speak into the device and the text will be written*
www.google.co.uk

### Speechify
*highlight text and it will be read aloud*
https://speechify.com

## MENTAL HEALTH SUPPORT
### Young Minds
*online mental health support*
www.youngminds.org.uk

### Heads Together
*a group of charities working together to support young people*
www.headstogether.org.uk

### Childline
*a phone line help centre where young people can talk to someone any time of the day or night*
www.childline.org.uk

## SLEEP
### Calm
*encouraging more restful sleep*
www.calm.com

### Headspace
*promoting relaxation techniques*
www.headspace.com

## ORGANISATION
### Brili
*create routines and schedules*
https://brili.com

### Trello
*manage projects and tasks*
https://trello.com

### Remember the Milk
*a to-do list that connects with your calendar*
www.rememberthemilk.com

## SEXUAL HEALTH SUPPORT
### Health for Teens
*everything a teenager wants to ask and know about their health*
www.healthforteens.co.uk

### Brook
*information about sex, sexuality and sexual health*
www.brook.org.uk

## EMOTIONS
### Kooth
*providing online emotional support*
www.kooth.com

## MONEY
### Monzo
*banking and managing money*
https://monzo.com

# Who Is Soli?

* Soli Lazarus founded Yellow Sun to support children and teenagers who have ADHD.

* Fully qualified teacher with 30 years' experience.

* Has an adult son with ADHD and so knows what it's like to struggle and feel isolated as a parent—whilst also loving the joy and unpredictability of her energetic son.

* Qualifications include Bachelor of Education Degree in Psychology, Life Coaching Diploma, Mental Health First Aid Practitioner.

* On the panel of Barnet Partnership for School Improvement.

* Former SENCO (Special Educational Needs Coordinator) at a large primary school in London.

* Writes a regular ADHD blog: www.soli-lazarus.com/blog

* Produces an ADHD podcast: www.anchor.fm/soli-lazarus

* Author of #1 Bestseller *ADHD Is Our Superpower*.

## Connect with Soli

🌐 www.soli-lazarus.com

✈ soli@yellow-sun.com

f @yellowsunsoli

𝕏 @soli_yellowsun

📷 soli_yellowsun

# Endnotes

1   Sun, H., Chen, Y., Huang, Q., Lui, S., Huang, X., Shi, Y., Xu, X., Sweeney, J. A., & Gong, Q. (2017). Psychoradiologic utility of MR imaging for diagnosis of attention deficit hyperactivity disorder: A radiomics analysis. *Radiology, 287*(2), 620–630. https://doi.org/10.1148/radiol.2017170226

2   Yogsan, J. (2013). Emotional maturity and adjustment in ADHD children. *Journal of Psychology & Psychotherapy, 3*(2), 114. https://www.longdom.org/open-access/emotional-maturity-and-adjustment-in-adhd-children-2161-0487.1000114.pdf

3   Cortese, S. (2020). Pharmacologic treatment of attention deficit–hyperactivity disorder. *New England Journal of Medicine, 383*(11), 1050–1056. https://doi.org/10.1056/NEJMra1917069

4   Hill, P. (2021). *The Parents' Guide to ADHD Medicines*. Jessica Kingsley Publishers.

5   Young, S., Moss, D., Sedgwick, O., Fridman, M., & Hodgkins, P. (2015). A meta-analysis of the prevalence of attention deficit hyperactivity disorder in incarcerated populations. *Psychological Medicine, 45*(2), 247–258. https://doi.org/10.1017/S0033291714000762

6   Albaugh, M. D., Ottino-Gonzalez, J., & Sidwell, A. (2021). Association of cannabis use during adolescence with neurodevelopment. *JAMA Psychiatry, 78*(9), 1031–1040. https://doi.org/10.1001/jamapsychiatry.2021.1258

7   Goriounova, N. A., & Mansvelder, H. D. (2012). Short- and long-term consequences of nicotine exposure during adolescence for prefrontal cortex neuronal network function. *Cold Spring Harbor Perspectives in Medicine, 2*(12), a012120. https://doi.org/10.1101/cshperspect.a012120

8   Chang, J., Su, K. P., Mondelli, V., Satyanarayanan, S. K., Yang, H. T., Chiang, Y. J., Chen, H. T., & Pariante, C. (2019). High-dose eicosapentaenoic acid (EPA) improves attention and vigilance in children and adolescents with attention deficit hyperactivity disorder (ADHD) and low endogenous EPA levels. *Translational Psychiatry, 9*(303). https://doi.org/10.1038/s41398-019-0633-0

9   Tarokh, L., Saletin, J. M., & Carskadon, M. A. (2016). Sleep in adolescence: physiology, cognition and mental health. *Neuroscience and Biobehavioral Reviews, 70*, 182–188. https://doi.org/10.1016/j.neubiorev.2016.08.008

10 Ofsted (2020). *The annual report of Her Majesty's Chief Inspector of Education, Children's Services and Skills 2018/19*. Her Majesty's Stationery Office, p. 87. https://assets.publishing.service.gov.uk/government/uploads/system/uploads/attachment_data/file/859422/Annual_Report_of_Her_Majesty_s_Chief_Inspector_of_Education__Children_s_Services_and_Skills_201819.pdf